THE WAY WE WERE

DOREEN McBRIDE

ADARE PRESS
White Gables
Ballymoney Hill
Banbridge
Telephone: (08206) 23782

Dedicated to the memory of a dear old friend Frances Shaw
with whom I had many hour's craic

Published by Adare Press
Typeset by December Publications
Printed by Banbridge Chronicle

ISBN 1 8994 96 05 X

CONTENTS

Family in mourning

I'M AWAY TO SEE A MAN ABOUT A DOG!

Old Sally rocked back and forth with gentle laughter. 'Child dear,' she exclaimed, 'you don't know you're living! Of course I've lived here all my life! And my parents and grandparents before me. You think this room is cramped? So it's only twelve feet square! Well, let me tell you, my parents raised fourteen children here. They slept on that bed against the wall and the children slept on bags of straw on the floor. We just lay down together and covered ourselves up with a couple of blankets. If the weather was very cold we threw our coats over us as well. Blankets with pockets, we used to call them.'

'Were you not cold on the floor?' asked Mary.

'No!' replied Sally, 'the fire was kept in. And we had plenty of turf cut from the bog. Do you see that turf cutter over there? It's never used now. I just keep it for sentimental reasons. Dad was a dab hand at wielding it. He used to cut enough turf in the summer to last a year. We piled it up in the bogs to dry out, then borrowed John Joe Jemmison's horse and cart to draw it down from the bog and stacked it against the gable wall. Heat was not a problem. This is a good solid house. It's built from stone and rubble. It's an entirely different kettle of fish from the mud cabins people had in the old days. Poor people used to build houses from turf or even sods cut out of the ground. Mud cabins leaked, soaked up water and fell apart after about ten

Turf was left to dry then brought by horse and cart
to be stacked against the gable wall

years so that their owners tried to prop them up using bits of wood or branches of trees. Many's the person died because their house collapsed on top of them and of course during the Great Hunger people died of starvation or famine fever, then were buried uncounted in unmarked graves when time caused their houses to fall around them.' 'That happened throughout Ireland, North, South, East and West.'

'That must have been an awful time,' John commented.

'Hunger, starvation, pestilence, helpless and hopeless in the face of death,' moaned Sally. 'We are descended from the survivors of a holocaust. I'm glad I was born in 1902, not 1800. I am now 94 years. If I'd been born a hundred years earlier I'd probably have starved to death between the years 1845 and 1847, that is, if I'd lived that long! At that time the average expectancy of life in Ireland was about 29 years. In the so called "good old days" people were nearly always in mourning, which meant they had to dress in black for a year. Once the mourning period was up somebody else in the family would pop off and the mourning gear would have to be resurrected. It was no joke!'

'Why did people die young?' asked Mary.

'Well, to begin with,' replied Sally, 'water supplies were dangerous and then medical science was not as advanced as it is today. People died of appendicitis, scarlet fever, diphtheria, pneumonia, tuberculosis and other diseases which are easily cured today. Also life was very unhygienic. Every September hundreds of babies took infantile diarrhoea and died because dirty houseflies covered their food with germs from the manure heap. People didn't know to keep them off food. It was as simple as that'.

'Now, please excuse me I'm away to see a man about a dog! The houseflies will be delighted.' Sally laughed, rose to her feet and disappeared out the door.

Traditional Irish Cottage

DON'T WASTE YOUR PIDDLE
ON THE HEDGE!

Ten minutes later shuffling footsteps were heard outside the door. Sally reappeared in the doorway, steadied herself on the doorpost, shambled into the cottage and took her place back on the chair in front of the fire.

'What did you mean saying you were away to 'see a man about a dog'? asked John.

Gales of laughter erupted from old Sally, tears of merriment ran down her cheeks.

'In the old days it was considered impolite to mention bodily functions to people you did not know well, so people would say things like "Excuse me while I go and turn the bike," or "I'm away to see a man about a dog."'

'That's peculiar!' laughed Mary and John.

'It was the custom,' replied Sally. 'By the way, where's my bathroom?'

'What do you mean? "Where's your bathroom?"' inquired John, looking around the two roomed cottage. It had only two doors, one leading to a small bedroom, the other outside. 'Where is your bathroom?'

Sally started laughing again. 'Come and I'll show you,' she chuckled. She led the way outside and stood proudly beside a thicket of bushes round the back of the house. 'That's my bathroom!' she proclaimed. 'If I need to do anything I do it in there, then I wash my hands at the pump over in the hedge near the door. Mind you, in the old days nobody would have thought of washing their hands. Water was too precious. And boys weren't allowed to disappear behind the bushes! Mother used to spin and dye wool. Most natural dyes are not fast. They need a substance called a mordant to make them stick to the cloth and mother used urine. She gathered lichens growing on the rocks down by the shore, soaked them in urine for about three months and made a lovely red dye which was used to colour flannel. People believed that boys' urine was stronger than girls' so she used to shout at the boys, "Don't waste your piddle on the hedge! Put it in the old pot behind the house." She was very cross if she found them disobeying! They were only allowed to disappear behind the bushes if they had a big job to do. We used the long grass instead of toilet paper. That could be dangerous! Poor wee

Spinning

Jamie once got a tick on his bottom from the long grass. It must have landed there off a cow. The poor wee soul was in agony. Ticks dig their heads into your skin and suck your blood. Jamie couldn't get it off by himself. Mother made him drop his pants and held a lighted match against the tick. Jamie screamed his head off, and the rest of the family were hysterical with laughter, but the tick fell away.'

'That's a terrible story!' gasped John, as he and Mary fell about giggling, 'Did all the people here just nip behind bushes?'

A lot of them did,' replied old Sally thoughtfully, 'But the Finlays, in that farm down the road, built themselves a seven seater wooden box in the byre, and they were not the only ones to do this.'

'A seven seater?' questioned Mary. 'Did seven people use it at one time?'

Seven seater toilet

'They could do!' exclaimed Sally, 'Many's the time I remember Bella saying, "I need to clock! Will anyone come with me to keep me company?" And a whole crowd would troupe through the door out of the kitchen into the byre. They'd sit there contentedly for ages having lovely wee conversations!'

'They all went together?' questioned Mary.

'Why not?' answered Sally. 'It's a perfectly natural bodily function. People are too prissy about the wrong things nowadays. Old Grandfather Finlay, he never went into the byre, he used to go behind the rhododendron bushes and they were never the same after he died. And I'll tell you worse than that. Tommy Blair used to hire an allotment on the outskirts of the town. A lot of people did that if they lived in terrace houses and had no land, or had a garden they considered too small. They used to grow fruit and vegetables for their families and either sell or give excess produce away. Tommy grew the best parsley in the neighbourhood by the simple expedient of piddling on it. He used to straddle a row of parsley and walk along dribbling on it. He didn't care who saw him!

'Now come and have a look at my bath.' She led the way to the old byre attached to the side of the house, went inside and pointed at a large zinc bath hanging on a nail.

Mary and John gazed in astonishment. 'That's your bath?' they gasped.

Sally went into gales of laughter again. 'I told you, you young ones are spoilt.' she chuckled. 'Yes! That's my bath. We were a clean family. We all used to have a bath every Saturday night, whether we needed it or not! We looked very respectable going to church on Sunday!'

'Gosh!' exclaimed Mary, 'In our house everybody has a bath or a shower every day!'

'I can believe it!' smiled Sally, 'All that bathing can't be good for you! You'll wash the natural oils off your skin! Seriously, in the old days water was a terrible problem. Every last drop had to be carried from the well. It was hard backbreaking work, so daily baths were not a proposition. Some people never bathed and on Sundays the skin underneath a nice clean white shirt was as black as your boot!

'We were lucky with our water supply. This is an isolated farmhouse and it's fairly high up the hill so I never knew the well's water to be contaminated. The soil will filter and purify waste coming from a few people, so we were alright, but it becomes clogged up and can't cope if too many people are performing there and it gets into the wells. Down in the village people used to become ill and die because they drank water from local pumps and wells. Epidemics of typhus and cholera swept the land. Even the wealthy did not escape. Queen Victoria's husband died in Windsor Castle from drinking

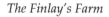

The Finlay's Farm

water which had been contaminated by sewage. In the old days there were no sewage pipes. People in towns had to use middens in streets. These were simply terrible, built in streets, open to public view and perhaps used by two hundred people. Each midden would have had a black, stinking stream flowing out of it and sewage soaked down through the soil and got into the water supplies. Then people drank it!'

'Ugh!' exclaimed Mary.

'"Ugh" indeed!' smiled Sally. 'Wealthy people looked better off, but they weren't really. They had servants to pump and carry water and they had water closets. The water closets looked very good, but there was nowhere for the sewage to go so it was collected in basements and pumped out onto the street at nights! Anyway, I was telling you about bathing, before I interrupted myself!

'Mother used to carry the bath into the house and place it in front of the fire, then she'd put a couple of buckets of water into it and heat it up by pouring a kettle of boiling water into it. She'd put more water on to boil and wash the youngest child, get it ready for bed and make it sit down quietly out of the way. She was very old-fashioned, was my mother so she'd put a small ember from the fire into the water to purify it for the next person. By the time she and Father had their bath the water looked like soup! Then the water was poured carefully down the drain. It wasn't fit for anything else! Water was always a problem. Remember, we had to collect it in buckets from the pump. There was no such thing as running water from taps in those days and carrying water was a slow heavy time-consuming job. As you can see I've had a sink with newfangled taps put in over there. It's made my life a lot easier.

It's great to have water which is safe to drink. You young ones wouldn't appreciate that, but I do and so do people in the third world.

'My grandmother emigrated to Belfast to find work. I remember her telling me about how in poverty-stricken areas of the town a water cart used to come round the streets and people got their supplies from that. The cart was nothing more or less than a gigantic barrel, filled with stinking liquid. She was given a glass of it once. She said there were twenty nine animals in that water which were big enough to see, never mind all the invisible ones! She reckoned if she had been stupid enough to drink it she would have sickened and died. She told me at that time all the rivers in Belfast were nothing more than open sewers and they used to flood and fill the houses along their banks with smelly slimy water. People living in those terrible conditions died in their thousands. It wasn't until the later half of the eighteenth century that the problem was cured with rivers like the Farset being encased in sewers.

'Many people got their water from stand pipes in the streets. The water wasn't always turned on and if you didn't manage to catch it when it was, you did without! There was an old crone in each street who took it upon herself to watch the stand pipe. When it was turned she used to shout her head off to attract attention and people came running with buckets to collect it. It was also smelly stuff, not fit for human consumption, but it was all the people knew. We were lucky on this farm. As far as I know we always had a reasonable water supply from our pump.

'We used to keep two buckets of water beside the door and we used it in a very economical fashion I'm telling you. We'd

nature. We have holes in the ozone layer, the greenhouse effect, a rising number of skin cancers and all sorts of harmful side effects. A bit of care and attention does no harm at all. The reason for doing something does not matter, the result does.

'Anyway, you're forgetting that in the past people did not have the advantage of modern scientific knowledge. Some of the terrible diseases which were prevalent at the time came on very quickly and changed their victim's appearance to such an extent they became unrecognisable. There was an old couple, Jamie John Jo Jemison and his wife Lizzie, who lived down the road. One day Jamie John Jo went out leaving Lizzie behind because she was not feeling well. When he came back he did not recognise her because she had typhus. He thought she was a changeling so he threw her into the fire. That's how changelings should be treated! It makes them disappear and the loved person reappears by magic. Poor old Lizzie was no changeling. She just had a blackened wizened face because she had typhus. She looked at Jamie John Jo as she died in the fire and asked "Why did you do that?" He, poor soul, was so upset he committed suicide.'

'How awful!' exclaimed Mary, 'But what's a changeling?'

'A changeling is a fairy left behind to take the place of somebody who's been stolen.

'Careful mothers never risked leaving their babies sleeping alone in their cradles without lifting the fire irons and putting them across the cradle to keep the fairies away. Fairies are thoughtless. They don't usually mean to do any harm. They are just a bit careless. If they like the look of a baby they'll steal it, take it away to fairyland and feed it magic food so that it forgets about its human connections. If you are ever stolen by the fairies, refuse all food. I'm warning you! Fairies sometimes steal grown ups. Young brides are at risk, but grown up changelings are comparatively rare, although I'd never risk going near an old place at night, just in case!'

'What's an old place?'

'An old fort or rath, a dolmen, or any other ancient site. Dangerous places they are! And so are fairy thorns. Keep away from them, especially at certain times of the year such as May eve and midsummer's night, when the fairies travel the earth in troupes stealing people, especially baby boys. In the old days boys were dressed like girls until they were about two years of age in order to confuse the fairies. The only way to tell the difference between fully clothed baby boys and girls was to look at their footwear. Girls had little button boots or shoes while boys had laces! My wee brother Arthur had lovely long ringlets when he was a baby! When he grew up I used to tease him!

'Arthur was a bit of a lad when he was young! He loved women, drinking and dancing. I'll never forget one night my mother woke up at about 2 o'clock. It was a fine

The Proleek Dolmen near Dundalk

Fairy Thorn

May night and she began to wail and cry. She woke the whole house up and made us get down on our knees and pray. Arthur's soul was in mortal danger, she said. He hadn't returned home from the dance. We thought he was just chasing women, but mother was in such a state we eventually took her seriously, knelt down beside her and began crying and praying for mercy. He appeared shortly after daylight and he was in a terrible state. He was pale and trembling and he had his coat on inside out. He said he was walking home after the dance past the Robinson's farm and he urgently needed to 'spend a penny'. He went into a field, did what he had to do and then he couldn't find the gate to get out. He walked round and round the field, but it didn't have a gate. He began to panic,

Arthur the night he escaped from the fairies

tied a handkerchief on the hedge as a marker and ran round the field. It did not have a gate. He remembered mother telling him that when the fairies are going to steal somebody they make the gates of fields disappear. By this time he was in a state of terror, but he tried to think cooly and recall everything mother told him about fairies. He said he was drunk when he went into the field but by this time he was cold stone sober from fright! He remembered mother telling us that if you think you're going to be stolen, eat human food and make yourself as ugly as possible by putting your coat on inside out. He was lucky because he found a bit of chocolate in his pocket, put a small piece in his mouth and ate it slowly. Then he put his coat on inside out and wandered around the field praying to the good Lord for mercy! The gate reappeared at dawn and he came home. He was a changed man! He became a pillar of the church and never touched a drop of drink again!'

'Do you really believe your brother was nearly stolen by the fairies? Or was he just the worse for drink?'

'I don't rightly know! All I do know is that in the past perfectly respectable people such as school teachers, priests, doctors and ministers reported hearing music coming from under the ground or thought they had seen the wee folk.'

'What do the fairies look like?' asked Mary.

'Not as you would expect!' smiled Sally. 'We do not have small dainty pretty fairies with wings in Ireland. Our fairies are usually ugly, old and wizened. They are about the same size as a two year old child. The most common ones are the leprechauns. They are often shoemakers and they keep a crock of gold at the foot of a rainbow! My cousin Lizzie's friend Maud Brown had a mother who thought her newborn daughter was a fairy. Poor wee Maud was a dwarf. Her arms and legs were too short. When she was born her mother asked the mid-wife to leave the baby beside the fairy fort so that the fairies could claim their own. Maud was lucky.

Maud Brown

The priest passed by, heard the baby crying and took her to the orphanage. I remember Maud saying she was a perfectly normal person inside an odd body! She did look a bit like a leprechaun!'

'Are leprechauns the only type of fairy?'

'Oh! Dear me no! There are many types of fairy. Cluricans are a sort of drunken leprechaun. They are very rare and are found drinking in rich men's cellars.

'The red cap is a nasty individual who plays practical jokes like throwing parcels of blood in your face. I don't like red caps!

'And then there is the far darrig, or man of hunger. This is a very thin individual who appears and begs for food. Granting his request brings good luck.

'My favourite fairy is the leanhaun shee. She is very beautiful and she loves men. If she manages to seduce a man he falls into her power, grows thinner and thinner and eventually dies. His poor soul has no peace, even beyond the grave. He is doomed to wander for eternity. The only way a man can escape from the clutches of the leanhaun shee is to get his best friend interested in her! However, the leanhaun shee has compensations. She inspires men to write beautiful poetry. They say that is why poets in Ireland tend to die young.'

'What's a banshee?' asked John.

'Ah! The poor banshee,' smiled Sally, 'she is a much maligned fairy. She is usually a woman who has died in tragic circumstances which have upset her to such an extent that she has remained near her family to warn them of impending death. She does not cause death, just acts as a warning by wailing and howling.

'AAAAhhhhhh!', Sally gave a shudder.

'What's wrong?' asked Mary.

'I'm just remembering the night I thought I heard a banshee. I didn't see anything. I just heard an awful eerie sound. It could have been a fox, but the strange thing is, young Ellen fell into the river and drowned a couple of days later. It makes you think.

'Banshees are only associated with the old families in Ireland and that usually means those whose surnames begin with an 'O' or an 'Mac' although I don't see why the poor woman could not follow a female line. I hate to think of banshees as sexist.'

'What about ghosts?' asked John.

'Ghosts are a fact of life.' replied Sally, 'They are the spirits of the dead. There is an old woman who haunts the road, down yonder, under those trees in front of the church. Matthew Finlay was driving along the road about 1934 in his wee car, it was an Austin Seven as far as I can remember. He passed under the trees and as he came out into the moonlight he chanced to look at the passenger seat. It was occupied! There was an old woman sitting in it. He had started out his journey alone and the shock of seeing her caused him to miss the bend at the bottom of the hill so he ended up in hospital. When he came round he asked about the woman. He was told the passenger seat was empty. He was stone cold sober at the time. It was said that the old woman had been killed by a horse and cart about 1916. She used to make fairly frequent appearances but I haven't heard of her lately. Perhaps she's gone to rest. AAAAAhhhhhh! The supernatural gives me the creeps as I feel as if a goose has walked on my grave. It is about time I made you a wee cup of tea in your hand.'

A WEE CUP OF TEA IN YOUR HAND

'How do you drink a cup of tea out of your hand?' asked Mary.

Sally went into gales of laughter. 'That's an old saying,' she replied, 'It means I'll give you a cup of tea and you can sit by the fire and drink it. I'm not going to lay the table. Would you like a wee bite?'

'No thank you!' shuddered John causing Sally to burst out laughing again.

'Another old saying?' questioned Mary.

'Correct!' replied Sally. 'You learn quickly! Would you like a wee bite means would you like a bite to eat? It doesn't mean I'm about to cannibalise you! Are you hungry?'

'I sure am!' laughed John.

'We must remedy that.'

Sally stood up and swung the crook outwards, lowered the kettle on the pot holder and swung it back again.

'In the old days,' she explained, 'everybody cooked using a crook and crane. Most crooks are set into the right side of the fire because most women are right handed. Do you see I can pull the crane towards me with my left hand and that leaves my right hand free to stir the contents of the pot. Traditionally the woman of the house sat on the right side of the fire, so that she could attend the crane, and the man sat on the left.

'In the old days we didn't have as much furniture as we do

24

today. I count myself lucky to have this fine upholstered chair. It's very comfortable. In the past we only had a couple of stick back chairs like the ones on which you're sitting and a clatter of creepie stools.'

'This stick back chair is surprisingly c o m f o r t a b l e .' commented John. 'What's a "creepie" stool?'

'A creepie stool is a three legged stool like that one

Fireplace with cook and crane, iron and goose wing

over there. The fact that it has only three legs means it sits steadily on an uneven floor. A four legged stool would rock. They were called creepie stools because babies used to learn to walk by pulling themselves upright beside the stool, then pushing it around.

'In the past people had different ideas from those common today about furniture arrangement. Furniture was arranged around the walls to keep the centre of the floor clear. That was important in a small room which was used by a lot of people. If the creepie stools had been placed in the middle of the floor

make an animal look more lively they used to stick a wee bit of ginger up its backside. That sure made a difference! William once had Harry harnessed up to take a load to market and the brute refused to move. In desperation father shouted to him to hold the reins tight and he stuck a bit of ginger in the right spot. Harry took off as if jet propelled and was through the gate and down the hill before you could say "Jack Robinson"! That ginger treatment sure was effective! So was tobacco, or a mouthful of turpentine blown into the correct place! I think I'd better toast us a bite of soda bread before you reckon I've rusted and need treatment!' She lifted an ornate metal stand from behind a pot, fixed it in front of the fire, sliced the soda bread lengthways and propped it on the stand.

'That's a handy gadget,' commented John.

'It is that!' replied Sally. 'It's called a harnen or bread stand. I use it to bake oat cakes and for making toast for visitors. If I'm just doing a wee slice for myself I'd use my toasting fork. There's nothing like the taste of bread toasted over the fire! It's crisp on the outside and soft inside. Delicious!

'You're lucky because yesterday I took the head staggers and made some butter. There's nothing like home-made butter for flavour and there's some raspberry jam left from last year.'

'How do you make butter?'

'Easy! I used to use that wooden churn standing in the corner and take my butter into market to sell. Now it's illegal to make your own butter to sell, something to do with laws of hygiene. Stuff and nonsense I say! If butter isn't made in a hygienic fashion it tastes awful and nobody in their right mind would buy it! The farmer down the road gives me cream. I need about four pints. I put it into that glass rotary churn and turn the handle and the butter appears as if by magic. I then pour the buttermilk off, remove the butter and shape it using those butter pats. Hard work but easy. Look! The kettle has boiled.' She swung the kettle towards her and poured a little water into it, swirled it about to warm the pot, then placed four teaspoons of tea into the pot, using the old formula, one for each person and one for the pot. 'John,' she requested, 'would you please pass me two mugs down from the dresser and that bowl at the end?'

John did as he was asked. 'What's the bowl for?' he questioned.

'That's very special,' replied Sally. 'It belonged to your great, great grandfather and I want you to drink from it. In the old days people didn't have a lot of crockery. If they were lucky each member of the family had a bowl. They began by eating their first course out of it, say soup and potatoes or Irish stew, then the bowl was wiped and the second course served, say stewed apples and custard after which the bowl was cleaned and used for drinking tea.'

'Do you mean to say ...... people did not have a different plate for each course?' gasped John.

'They were lucky to have a bowl,' replied Sally. 'I've heard of people who didn't have any crockery at all at all. They just ate potatoes by holding them in their hands. I heard of one destitute family of four who were rightly flummoxed during the famine when they were given a little Indian corn which they used to make a thin gruel. They couldn't eat that out of their hands so dug four holes in their clay floor, filled them with gruel and kept body and soul together by lapping like dogs.'

'That's awful!'

'It was awful,' replied Sally, 'Now eat up some of my good soda bread.'

'It's delicious!' exclaimed Mary. She looked with interest at the pots lined up along the fireplace. 'You've a right lot of pots!'

'I have indeed!' giggled Sally. 'In the old days you could tell how wealthy a household was by the number of pots owned. Unfortunately I don't have a lot of money. I just inherited pots from people who died off. That big pot there holds 25 gallons of water. Big Aggie used to boil her wash in that every Monday. Mother used to use that smaller pot to boil potatoes for the family. She also did the washing in it on Mondays so we ate leftovers from Sunday, or poked potatoes and onions into the fire to cook.'

Family group

'Did they not become all black and burnt?' asked John.

'They were black and burnt on the outside but once we'd peeled the skin off they were delicious,' replied Sally.' Do you see that pot with the flat bottom and lid? That's a pot oven. We used to poke a bit of the fire out onto the hearth, place the pot oven on top of it, put soda bread or wheaten bread inside, pop the top on and place a few embers on top and bake the bread.'

How do you make potato bread?' asked Mary.

'Simple!' replied Sally. 'Mash some cooked potatoes up with a little flour and some milk to make a stiff dough, roll it out with a rolling pin and bake it on this flat iron thing, called a griddle, over the fire. I used to make pancakes and drop scones on the griddle as well'.

'It sounds as if the fire was of vital importance,' commented Mary.

'It was indeed!' laughed Sally. 'It acted as a source of heat, it warmed water and was a main source of light in the days when there was no electricity and candles and oil lamps were thought expensive to run. And it was a great place to gather round for a ceilli evening.'

'A ceilli?' questioned Mary, 'What in heaven's name is a ceilli?'

COME AND CEILLI

Old Sally stretched her wrinkled hand into her pocket, drew out a mouth organ, placed it between her lips and began to play a lively gig.

Mary and John gazed at her in disbelief. 'Where did you learn to do that?' they gasped.

'I just kind of picked it up,' replied Sally. My brothers used to play the mouth organ. Why I remember the night Enie competed in the Ulster Hall. He played 'Rhapsody in Blue' and he played it beautifully. Put his whole soul into it he did. He felt he should have won First Prize, but the judge thought differently and placed him second. Enie was so disgusted he never played the mouth organ after that and I inherited his instrument. I used to go into the barn to practise. Enie said I wasn't bad at playing, certainly I was in demand at ceilli evenings. This was a ceilli house you know.'

'What's a ceilli?' repeated Mary, 'And how do you spell it?'

'Ceillis are fun!' laughed Sally, 'Many's the good time we had here! Ceilli is pronounced 'kayley', but spelt ceilli, or if you would prefer the older spelling, ceilidhe'. It simply means making your own entertainment at home, having craic, or fun, together. People tended to congregate here and ceilli, that's how it came to be known as a ceilli house. In the old days there must have been a hundred ceilli houses in the neighbourhood.

People would just drop in, Old Willie brought his fiddle, granny told stories, Mother used to sing, Father played the bones, Arthur was a mean hand on the boran, I used to play my mouth organ, or whistle. It was unusual for a girl to be a whistler so I was in great demand at local concerts. Carrie used to gub, that means make faces. She was very funny. Enie played the accordion, when he gave up the mouth organ while Eric and Sam tootled away at the flute. Television spoilt all

Accordion player

that although sometimes people round here switch it off, put out the word and ceilli in the old style.'

'Please Sally,' pleaded John, 'whistle us a tune, something you'd have done in the old days.'

'I'm not sure that I can still whistle,' smiled Sally, 'Still I'll give it a go,' she pursed up her mouth and after a few false starts gave a startling rendition of 'The Lark in The Clear Air.' Mary and John sat entranced as the sweet high notes soared throughout the house. 'That was wonderful,' they breathed when Sally had finished.

'Whistling's all right,' stated Sally emphatically, but I really loved my mouth organ. I would have loved to play it on the Twelfth of July in the Orange parade, but they had nothing but flute bands around here so I never got the opportunity. I used to envy Sam and Eric marching on the Twelfth!'

'I loved our Twelfth of July celebrations. To be deprived of the "Twelfth" was unthinkable! It would have been like doing without Christmas! The whole community used to turn out in force and we had a great time. We used to lend our drums to the people marching on St. Patrick's day. Many's the drum wore the shamrock on 17th March then followed that experience up by being decorated with orange lilies on 'The Twelfth.' It's impossible for the uninitiated to tell the difference between a Hibernian band and an Orange one. They have similar banners, similar dress and play similar music. Sometimes my brothers played with the Hibernians on St. Patrick's day. That's the way it should be. In this neighbourhood, at any rate, what polarisation there is happened recently, due to our present 'troubles' and it spoilt a lot of fun.

'The eleventh night was exciting with folk coming and going, other things like the opening of the Orange Hall and discussing the bus timetables. My brothers played in a Silver Band so their instruments had to be cleaned and the girls were responsible for ironing trousers and shirts of their uniforms.

'Ironing was difficult because our old-fashioned iron did not run off electricity. We had to fish a rectangular piece of metal out of the iron, push it into the fire until it became red hot, remove it, stick it back into the iron and smooth away until the iron became cold again, when we repeated the whole process. I hated ironing because I always managed to end up with my hands covered with burns.

'We used to go for a walk about 7 o'clock, visiting neighbours, seeing their preparations, the cleaning of instruments, the clothes grooming and the important task of cleaning and mending the lodge banner and tying on black bows as a mark of respect if a member had died during the year, and so on. Personally I prefer the banners the Blacks have to the Orange ones because they are all Biblical scenes. The Blacks walk on 13th July and their parades are smaller and generally quieter than the Orange ones. Anyway the Halls looked after the Black banner. They lived in a wee house in Main Street and were strict Presbyterians, you know the sort, really kindly people who went to church twice on Sundays and 'holy' meetings during the week. They would not let alcohol pass their lips and they never went to dances. We used to say that Presbyterians would never make love standing up in case they enjoyed it and began to dance! Do you get the general picture of God fearing, good living, narrow minded people? Well the first time I saw that banner I nearly died. The 'Thirteenth' had been wet. That day the rain came down in stair-rods so it did! The banner was soaked and was hung up to dry suspended from the Halls' parlour ceiling. The banner depicted Adam and Eve in the garden of Eden. Both were stark staring naked and Eve had a shelf of a bosom. In other circumstances I am convinced the Halls would have been shocked by that painting, but because it was on the banner it passed muster! It sure was an overpowering sight in the parlour and to this day pictures of nudes are a rare sight in working class homes in Ireland!'

'On the 'Eleventh' night we always called for Theresa O'Flynn. She was my best friend and I often went to Mass with her. She had a great time teaching me to genuflect, but I digress. Together we went down into the village and walked up Main Street admiring the decorative arch, the bunting and the Union Jack flags which hung from most of the houses. It was fun! Groups of people craiced about past years and there were small unofficial practice walks by bands and men playing the Lambeg drums. That's a sound to stir the blood! I loved

Lambeg drums.
That's a sound to stir the blood!

watching those big men struggling under the weight of those huge drums with the sweat dripping off their brows as they bate the hell out of it! I've often wondered why the Lambeg drum is accompanied by flute? It doesn't seem to make sense. Anyway, the celebration was a folk festival enjoyed by all, in this part of the country at any rate.

'Then there was the bonfire! The local lads began to collect material for it about the beginning of June. In the old days they used to cut down small trees and drag them up the street to the waste piece of land on which they built the bonfire. Thankfully that practice has been stopped. It is illegal now so the bonfire is built from rubbish people have thrown out. It was lit after dark by a local dressed up as King Billy.'

'Who was King Billy?' queried John.

'Why William of Orange, of course,' relied Sally, with a twinkle in her eye. 'He was Catholic King James's son-in-law.

He married King James's daughter Mary and became embroiled in a war which involved the whole of Europe. The rest of Europe appears to have forgotten about it, but we haven't!

'Was it a struggle between Catholicism and Protestantism?' asked Mary.

'Not quite,' replied Sally. 'That was certainly an element but the Pope was an unofficial supporter of King Billy! That's a fact that's mostly forgotten here!

'The town names which appear on arches and banners commemorate battles, "Derry, Aughrim, Enniskillen and the Boyne!" The battle of the Boyne, when King Billy finally defeated King James, took place in 1690, hence the slogan "Remember 1690!"'

'Is that why some places have walls painted with a man on a white horse?' asked Mary.

'That's right dear,' replied Sally. 'There's a great tradition of wall painting throughout Ireland. It takes different forms in different places.'

'Tell us more about the Twelfth,' requested John.

'In the past it was more of a joke and a folk festival than it is today. Our Willie used to go and stand by the hedge next to the Logue's house. They were Roman Catholics, you know. He took a wooden spoon and a bin lid with him and sang 'Here comes the Pope with a shovel up his coat.' On St. Patrick's Day Sean Logue used to appear at the other side of the hedge, complete with spoon and bin lid and sing to Willie. Then the pair would go up the pub together and have a drink. We really missed the carousing when Sean died!'

'There was a wonderful carnival atmosphere on the Eleventh night. The bonfire was huge and the craic was mighty! We used to sit on that rise up from the bonfire site, sing party songs and cheer whenever something was thrown on the fire causing it to blaze up. People danced in the street and a good time was had by all. Sometimes the dawn was beginning to break before we went to bed. It took stamina to survive the "Twelfth" celebrations, I'm telling you!

'On the morning of the "Twelfth" itself we girls got out of bed early, lit the fire and had a quick cup of tea, then cleared out of the way so that the band members could titivate. No member of the human race needs more time to dress than a fellow preparing to play in a band! The girls, weather permitting, went and sat on the dry stone wall opposite the door, looking forward to the dance which followed the procession, gossiping and chatting about our plans for the day, the fellows we hoped to see and so on. Then we made our way down to the village and congregated at the local Orange hall to catch the bus which was waiting to take us to a larger village or town for the Orange parade.

'The bus was full of excitement, banners, instruments, drums and flags. It was standing room only for children. We squeezed on and were usually given a shove up to the front by one of the officials. I thought it was just great! I was filled full of pride by our band, the smart appearance of my brothers in their uniforms and the village Orange men with their dark suits, orange sashes and hard bowler hats. I always had a marvellous time dandering about and chatting to people.

'We arrived back at the Orange Hall in the village about seven o'clock when the band completed its last march of the day and we made our way to the church hall for tea.

'The church had a big silver tea urn. Tea bags had not been invented in those days so the Vicar's wife threw tea leaves into the urn along with milk and sugar and boiled the whole lot together. We drank the resulting sweet milky tea out of thick, white cups. If anybody didn't take milk and sugar it was tough titty because there was no choice! We ate big, thick doorsteps of sandwiches made from cornbeef or tomato, followed by a small cake or biscuit.

'The church hall was tidied up when we finished eating. We washed the dishes, brushed the floor and the dance commenced. We all joined in and danced the 'lancers', foxtrots, waltzes, the 'Pride of Erin', quicksteps, the Gay Gordons, tangos and other dances in vogue at the time. My favourite was the 'Moonlight Saunter'! It was very different from today's disco dancing where all people seem to do is stand and wiggle at each other. And the music wasn't too loud! You could have a conversation and your ears weren't left ringing! Mind you, by this time some of the brethren had been drinking steadily all day, were quite merry and got the dances mixed up! It was all good fun. When the dance ended between 11 and 12 o'clock when the band played 'God Save the Queen' and we went into fits of giggles because some of the brethren had so much drink taken they had difficulty standing up to attention while the national anthem was being played. Our laughter was rewarded by glares from sober lodge members because of our lack of respect.'

'Were ceillis, St. Patrick's Day and the 'Twelfth' celebrations the only type of entertainment you had?' asked John.

'Oh dear no!' smiled Sally. 'We had dances in the village hall every Saturday night. That was a great place to meet the local talent although some of the lads were terrible tricksters. I'll never forget the night poor Cissie Curran had the life scared out of her! We used to dance downstairs, then about halfway through the evening there was an interval and the girls went upstairs to refresh themselves and to use the chamber pots. The hall did not have either a ladies or a gents cloakroom so the boys disappeared behind the hall, if necessary, and the girls used a row of chamber pots lined against the wall upstairs. Well, on the night in question big Ernie Scott, who was the biggest lig in creation, put a pinch of Andrews Liver salts into each chamber pot. Of course when the girls used them the salts foamed away up around their backsides! Cissie was easily excited. She was so shocked she screamed, then fainted and had to be carried outside!

'Sometimes we had boxing contests in the hall. They were exciting, especially if a champion was hired to take on the local fellows. Alex Gibson fancied himself as a boxer. He volunteered to take on the visiting champion and spent the week before hand boasting about what he would do with his winnings. The great day, or should I say night, arrived. Alex got on his gear, climbed into the ring and the big brawny champion made a swing at him. Alex was so scared at the sight of the champion his bowels moved and he made a terrible mess of himself. Some wag from the back shouted, "Look! Yer man's lost his gum shield!"

'On a different tack there were gospel meetings in the village square. Hundreds of people used to stand around in a circle enjoying a hellfire and thunder preacher who would shout about the importance of being "born again". I'll never forget the day when a preacher shouted "Ye must be born again" and a voice from the back yelled "A man born in Derry doesn't need to be born again!" or the day when Andy McFadden was supposed to make his testament because he had been "saved"! Andy was very nervous so he took a few drinks to steady his nerves and rolled on centre stage. The preacher asked if he had been saved and how did he feel. Andy, who was one over the eight, replied at the top of his voice "I feel so ****ing good I could put my ****ing foot through a ****ing Lambeg drum!

'The mummers, or 'straw men' used to appear around Christmas, especially on 26th December, and at weddings. They came disguised in masks, made a lot of noise, performed a little play, collected some money and disappeared as quickly as they had come. They gave us a tune or two and left us with our feet tapping. 'I wonder if I can remember a few of the old tunes. Hold on while I see if I can give them a go. I need to cheer myself up. There's a lot of wonderful things about life today, but I feel sad that the good old ceilli evenings have nearly disappeared, that the mummers are nearly extinct, there's no more dancing or boxing in the local hall and the Twelfth has become so political. There was a lot to be said for the way we were!

Mummer